Contents

chapter 1: whitewater

Today 6

History 8

chapter 2: the water

Difficulty 12

Grades 14

River types 16

chapter 3: whitewater sports

Adventure 20

Expedition 22

Solo kayaking 26

Rafting 28

Rafting competitions 30

Creeking 32

Freestyle 34

Slalom 36

Squirt boating 38

chapter 4: the gear

Safety 42

Clothing 44

On the water 46

chapter 5: people and places

Hot spots 50

Shaun Baker 52

Amazing paddlers 54

Young talent 56

Joey's story 58

Milestones 60

Glossary 62

Index 64

chapter 1: whitewater

4

Steve Fisher, one of the greatest whitewater paddlers ever, heads towards a massive hole on the Zambezi River's famous rapid number nine in Zambia.

Whitewater makes for some truly global sports. Rafting and kayaking are practised all over the world, from New Zealand and China to Iceland and Iran. They let individuals explore the unique, and often secret, world of rivers.

Paddlers explore all types of whitewater. Some surf big waves doing aerial tricks. Others enjoy expeditions, such as ten days in the Himalayas carrying all their equipment in their kayaks. Paddlers even run some of the world's largest waterfalls that are tourist attractions. The opportunities are countless.

Whitewater kayaking is a sport that attracts all types of people – men, women, young and old

Wherever there are rivers, there are paddlers searching for the ultimate whitewater experience

Individuals adapt to their dynamic environment using skills and knowledge. Any whitewater sport can be dangerous, so proper instruction and guidance is a must. There are many kayak schools offering superb courses.

The key ingredients for whitewater sports are water and air. When water moves quickly over rocks in a steep river, air gets trapped in the water causing it to look white. The stage is now set for a lot of fun!

Water is an incredibly strong element, and any whitewater paddler needs a lot of training to master it

7

Today, people paddle for pleasure, but thousands of years ago these skills were crucial to survival. North and South American Indians, along with the Polynesian islanders of the Pacific, used canoes for hunting, fishing and travel.

Early canoes

Ancient rafts and canoes were made from a variety of natural materials, such as reed. Indeed, reed canoes are still being used today on the Nile River in Egypt and on Lake Titicaca, bordering Bolivia and Peru. The oldest known canoe was found in the tomb of a Sumerian king near the River Euphrates. This raft is estimated to be about 6,000 years old. Though canoes are still in use today, they are not very popular for whitewater sports.

A traditional reed raft on Lake Titicaca

For survival

Inuits of the Arctic developed what is called a closed-cockpit kayak. Covering, or closing, the top of the kayak stopped the icy waters of the Arctic Ocean from filling the kayak. The Inuits' kayaks had whalebone and driftwood frames, with sea lion skin stretched tightly over them. The whole thing was waterproofed with whale fat. An Inuit's kayak was their lifeline, allowing them to hunt and fish every day.

For sport

It was John MacGregor, a British barrister, who popularised canoeing as sport among the middle classes of Europe and the USA in the late 19th century. He designed a boat similar to the closed-cockpit kayaks used by the Inuits.

John MacGregor canoeing through Tuttlingen, Germany

Many paddlers set out on long treks just to find the perfect whitewater. This group are exploring the canyon on the Upper Mendoza River, Argentina.

Knowing how tough a stretch of water is going to be is vital info for any paddler. There are six grades, or classes, used to describe water, with the easiest being Grade 1. The highest, grade 6 is so difficult that only the most experienced paddlers can survive it.

The international scale of river difficulty grades water on both the technical difficulty and the danger associated with a stretch of river, or single rapid. It also gives the paddler an idea what skill level is required to undertake this particular section of water.

Picking a route through the Soca River, Slovenia

Kayaker Erik Martinsonn descends into the white foam of the Ulvua River, Norway

The grades vary a lot, for example there can be a hard Grade 2, easy Grade 3 or hard Grade 5. The grade of a river or a rapid can change as the water level changes, such as after heavy rain or when mountain snow melts in spring.

More water usually makes rapids more powerful and difficult, although they can become easier if the water covers hazards such as boulders. When a river is in flood stage, or 'spate', the fast-flowing water can have a lot of pressure, and be very dangerous. Flooded rivers are also extremely hazardous to navigate, so should only be undertaken by expert paddlers. If a kayaker happens to exit their kayak in a flooded river, rescuing them and their equipment can be a dangerous operation.

Exit a kayak Fall out of the kayak into the water

For paddlers, matching their skills to the water's grade means getting to grips with terms such as boil, whirlpool, ledge and drop. Not just that, but paddlers need to know if they're up to the grade before getting on the water.

Grade 1

This is easy whitewater, with a regular current, small waves and simple obstacles to navigate.

Grade 2

This grade has fairly difficult whitewater, with clear, open passages. The current can change, with medium-sized waves, holes and obstacles to navigate round.

Grade 3

This is difficult whitewater! The passage is clear but has high waves, holes and boils, not to mention boulders and other obstacles.

Grade 4

At this grade the paddler needs to get out of the boat to find a clear line if in a rapid. The water pressure is strong with big waves, strong holes, boils, whirlpools, boulders, ledges and drops.

Grade 5

This whitewater is extremely difficult. Each rapid needs careful thought as often the only safe route is very narrow. High waves with strong holes and pressure areas are some of the challenges that the paddler will meet.

Grade 6

By now, the paddler is at the limit! Grade 6 is usually only possible to navigate at certain water levels and even then it is extremely dangerous and can be life-threatening. It is only for experienced professionals.

Boil A place in the water where two currents meet; the pressure of both currents is very strong, which makes for a powerful collision and masses of whitewater

Boulder A large rock

Drop Any spot where flowing water drops suddenly, possibly creating a waterfall

Hole A feature in the river where turbulent water returns on itself, creating a hydraulic. Some holes can be life-threatening.

Ledge The upper lip or edge of a drop

Rapid A section of a river where the river bed is relatively steep, which increases the speed and turbulence of the water flow

Whirlpool A swirling body of water under the water's surface

Pool drop

Pool drop rivers have equal measures of rapids and calmer water. After each rapid, the water pools out at the bottom, making them great for people learning to paddle. Many of these rivers are found in Norway and California, USA.

Alpine

These rivers aren't for beginners, but are amazing fun for competent paddlers. They drop very quickly in height, so are very steep with fast-flowing water, making it hard to stop sometimes.

Volume The amount of water in the river

High-volume

Although they may not have much gradient, these wide rivers gather their water from a large area, so they end up with big, bouncy rapids and really good surfing waves. They also tend to have fewer obstacles and be masses of fun! The Nile and Zambezi Rivers in Africa have become a home for freestyle kayakers wanting to perfect their acrobatic tricks on big waves.

Steep creeks

These slim rivers, as the name says, are extremely steep, lower-volume and narrow, with lots of little drops, waterfalls and slides. The riverbed is often bedrock. There are a lot of fun steep creeks in the northern part of the Italian Alps, as well as California, USA.

chapter 3:

whitewater sports

British freestyling pro Matt Cooke enjoys some paddling on the impressive Falls of Lora, Scotland.

Whitewater river running is all about sharing exciting adventures that test paddlers' skills as they make their way safely to the bottom of a river. For some, it could be paddling a Grade 1 river, while others live for the buzz of a Grade 5 creek!

A pair of paddlers exploring the San Giovanni River, Italy

Whitewater kayaking in a remote part of the world, with a small group of friends, gives paddlers an amazing sense of freedom

Running a whitewater river safely relies on teamwork, strategy and careful planning. Paddlers usually go out in groups of at least three people so they can work as a team, keeping each other safe. Together, the paddlers break down their route into a series of individual challenges that can be tackled safely by working as a unit. Clear communication is vital. The roaring water means that hand signals are the only sure way of getting a message across.

River running has advanced massively since the early days of the sport. Strong plastic kayaks give paddlers lots of control and keep them safe. Paddlers now use a dynamic and athletic style of paddling, as well as better techniques, meaning they have more control than ever. This is pushing river running to new heights.

Sophisticated kayaks allow pros like British Andy Phillips to master even the trickiest of passages

The huge and overwhelming water masses of the River Indus, Pakistan

Expedition kayaking has been called the ultimate whitewater adventure. Negotiating the course of an unknown river takes skill, knowledge and planning, so only the most determined kayakers can pull it off.

Whitewater expeditions usually take place in remote areas of the world. The rivers are set in dense jungles, hidden canyons or high mountain ranges. Often the only way to reach these remote rivers is by kayak, which makes expedition kayaking so unique. An expedition demands real commitment as it can take days to follow the river through challenging terrain. Usually only a small, dedicated team of up to four people can complete such an undertaking.

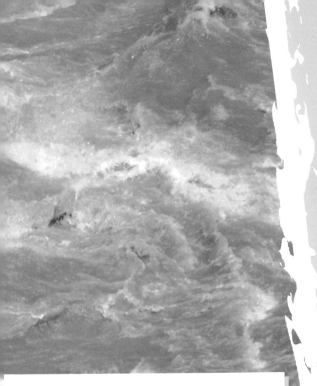

WHITEWATER

The Bachrati River in Iran's Zagros mountains is one of the world's most impressive canyons

Expedition kayakers take a range of equipment with them, such as:

- video and photographic equipment
- sleeping bags and mats
- tents
- cooking pans and stoves
- all their food
- satellite phone and maps
- spare paddles
- rescue equipment
- clothes

Camping out on the banks of the Kanali River, Nepal

Paddlers use normal whitewater kayaks but cleverly store their supplies and equipment in the spaces under and behind their seats, as well as in the front by their foot rests. Waterproof bags are used to keep everything dry.

Intrepid kayakers have undertaken some incredible whitewater expeditions over the years. In modern times, these range from the heroic descent of the Blue Nile River to what is probably the greatest kayak expedition of our time – the Tsangpo Expedition.

Blue Nile waterfalls near Bahir Dar, Ethiopia (Africa)

Blue Nile River

In 1972, Mike Jones and Mick Hopkinson from Britain led the alpine descent of the Blue Nile River in Ethiopia, running a longer section of the river, with much bigger rapids, than had ever been done before. During the expedition, the group encountered Nile crocodiles, ferocious hippos, dangerous rapids and unfriendly tribespeople.

Tsangpo expedition

In 2002, American expedition paddler Scott Lindgren led a 96-strong team on the first descent of the Tsangpo Gorge in Tibet. It took place during the depths of the freezing Himalayan winter, when the river's waters were at their lowest level. At its core, the team had seven international paddlers with a wealth of experience and expertise in river exploration.

Scott Lindgren scouts a section of rapids on the Tsangpo River

The team at Tsangpo River, Tibet, 2002; the paddlers are, from left to right, Johnnie Kern, Allan Ellard, Mike Abbott, Willie Kern, Scott Lindgren, Dustin Knapp, Steve Fisher

The mighty Tsangpo Gorge is the deepest river gorge in the world. By entering it, Scott and his team made kayaking history. Their expedition was a complete success. They explored further into the gorge than anyone else before them. The team had raised the bar in expedition paddling.

Alpine descent A steep river with fast-flowing water

On 10 April 2007, South African kayaker Hendri Cortez set out to paddle the Murchison Falls section – one of the most dangerous sections of any river in the world. His goal was to complete this notorious, 80-kilometre stretch of the White Nile River in Uganda on his own!

Hendri Cortez knew what he was taking on. The Murchison Falls section of the White Nile River – famous for its extreme whitewater – had only ever been successfully kayaked four times. Three of those trips were by Hendri and his team. So he knew, more than anyone else, the dangers he faced. He would be exposed to treacherous rapids and dangerous wildlife.

Hendri had to make sure his equipment was absolutely intact, as his life depended on it

The view from just below the Murchison Falls

Murchison Falls isn't just famed for its whitewater, but also for the wild animals found there. There are more hippos in this stretch of river than anywhere else in the world. Hippos are known to aggressively defend their territory, and they can be even more dangerous than crocodiles! Hendri paddled fast, concentrating on every piece of water, dodging all the dangers to complete this amazing feat in just two days.

Hendri had to move carefully to avoid the agressive nature of the native hippos

Hendri had to prove himself in many Grade 5 rapids, like this one

Whitewater rafting is the perfect activity for anyone with a sense of adventure who is looking for an exciting physical challenge. Led by experienced guides, groups in inflatable rubber rafts ride hair-raising rapids on some of our planet's greatest rivers.

Rafting is probably the oldest method of river transport in the world. For thousands of years, people have used rafts to carry food and essential supplies. As a recreational sport, whitewater rafting grew in popularity during the late 1970s. Nowadays, it is more popular than ever with rafting companies in countries from Indonesia to Iceland offering expeditions.

Preparing for the big drop,
Zambezi River, Zambia

WHITEWATER

A view of the impressive
Karakoram Mountains from
the Indus River, Pakistan

Rafting provides an amazing
experience for a team of people

Raft trips offer amazing experiences.
Imagine travelling down the mighty Zambezi
River in Africa for seven days. The only
people to be seen on the journey are local
villagers collecting water and fishermen
catching their dinner from the river.

The American river explorer,
Richard Bangs, led pioneering
expeditions during the late
1970s and 1980s that
opened up some of the
world's greatest rivers.

Here are just a few places
that now offer whitewater
rafting experiences – all
thanks to Richard's sense
of adventure!

- Indus River, Pakistan

- Omo River, Ethiopia

- Yangtze River, China

Brazil vs Japan in the
2007 World Rafting
Championships sprint

It was not until the 1990s that rafting became included in major game events, but since then it has grown quickly in popularity. Countries from around the world began competing in various disciplines, and in 1998 these events became World Championships. Rafting competitions consist of three disciplines: sprint, slalom and downriver. The points from each are added together to determine the overall winner. Each team has six members with the option to have a reserve.

Sprint

The sprint is the most visually exciting discipline and counts for 30 per cent of the points. It is an elimination race in which pairs of teams race down a section of powerful rapids.

Elimination race A race which consists of heats of pairs racing down rapids. The winner of each heat proceeds to the next round with two teams remain for the final

Brazil in the 2003 slalom event

Slalom

The Slalom is the most technically challenging discipline and counts for 30 per cent of the points. High levels of technique and teamwork are needed to negotiate through twelve downriver and upriver gates in rapids. Touching, failing to pass, or intentionally moving a gate results in a penalty.

Israel and South Africa in the 2001 downriver event on the Zambezi River

Downriver

The downriver event is worth 40 per cent of the points. The race is close to an hour of racing along a section of continuous and powerful rapids. Technical ability and endurance are essential elements to ensure a good position in this event. The points earned by the teams in the previous events determine their position in the starting line up in groups of up to five rafts.

A revolution in boat design made the sport of creek boating possible. Until the mid-1980s, paddlers used long, fragile, fibreglass boats. The Topolino kayak changed all that – and the sport has never looked back.

Creek boating is the most extreme form of kayaking. It involves paddling down very steep waterfalls and low water volume creeks. Long boats were extremely difficult to manoeuvre on these steep, rocky rivers. The small, specially-designed Topolino is just 2.2 metres long, making it ideal for creeking. Creek boats need to be short and manoeuvrable so they are buoyant and sit well on the water surface.

Ripping waterfalls, such as this one in Norway, can only be mastered in an extremely manoeuvrable kayak

British pro kayaker Shaun Baker mastering the Rauma River, Norway, in his Topolino

Boats with rounded ends, like the Topolino are also less likely to get stuck on underwater rocks when paddlers jump off waterfalls and drops.

Paddlers learned from sports such as skiing and mountain biking how to cope with the impact of landing after a big drop. Paddlers found they needed to make their bodies absorb the shock – like a spring. By positioning themselves forwards as they land, they can absorb most of the impact energy through their bodies. If they don't do this they can break lots of bones.

Extreme kayaking races include many big drops, like this one on **Upper Cherry Creek, California, USA**

Freestyle kayaking is the youngest whitewater sport. Playboating, as it is often called, is a gymnastic form of kayaking. Paddlers perform trick after trick, each requiring the highest levels of precision, technique, balance, coordination and spatial awareness.

Static water

Freestyle kayakers perform their tricks on a static piece of water, like a hole. This means that the shape and size of the hole stay the same. The kayakers use small, agile kayaks with a concentrated volume, that can be popped into the air easily. Most freestyle kayaking is done on just a small stretch of water, allowing paddlers repeated opportunities to improve their skills.

Concentrated volume The volume of a kayak that lends it maximum buoyancy

Play runs

Most rivers used for freestyle have small sections known to local paddlers as 'play runs'. They consist of various waves and holes where paddlers can practice their latest moves.

Championships

Every two years, freestylers from all over the world compete at the World Freestyle Championships at varying locations all around the world. There are 98 competitors (both male and female) and 36 junior competitors (under 18). Each paddler has 45 seconds to perform their chosen moves, and gets the highest scores for difficulty of moves, combinations and managing to jump completely out of the water.

Whitewater slalom racing isn't just a battle with the river, but also a race against the clock. The competitors negotiate a series of gates on the river, each of which they must pass through. It is one of the very few whitewater disciplines in which competing teams use canoes.

A French crew go for gold on the finish line at the 2006 European Slalom Championships, France

Slalom gates are two poles hung from wires over the river. They are coloured as either green (downstream) or red (upstream), indicating the direction they must be negotiated in. Upstream gates mean the paddler has to go against the current to pass the gate, then proceed down-stream again. Most slalom courses take 80 to 120 seconds to complete for the fastest paddlers. Paddlers compete in teams or solo, and time penalties are given if paddlers miss gates or touch them. Precision is the key to successfully competing in whitewater slalom.

Paddling together as a two-person team, or crew, is quite hard work. Each paddler needs to know exactly what the other is doing to keep the boat precisely on course. The paddler at the back steers the direction of the boat, while the front man is mostly responsible for the boat's speed.

Scottish Olympic silver medallist, Campbell Walsh, at the 2006 European Slalom Championships, France

Whitewater slalom racing is an Olympic sport. Competitors at the Olympic slalom races use sleek, carbon fibre kayaks that are 3.5 metres long and weigh 10 kilograms. Paddlers race down 300 m of whitewater through 20 to 25 gates. Olympic runs take fast paddlers about 140 seconds to complete. Other international slalom competitions include the European and World Championships and the World Cup. European paddlers dominate the sport at international level, which isn't surprising given that kayaking is the national sport of Slovakia and hugely popular throughout in Europe.

37

Squirt boating evolved when slalom racers started to dip the stern of their boat under the water's surface. This new manoeuvre was named a tail squirt. Paddlers started to develop this new technique until they were able to get their boats vertical.

Squirt boater performing a Cartwheel

Squirt boaters use both the river's surface and underwater currents. Paddlers perform tricks, like Cartwheels where the boat is rotated vertically from end to end. The Mystery Move is where the paddler disappears completely underwater, though still travels along in full control. Paddlers use these squirt boating tricks to expand their skills in whitewater and improve their control over their boat.

Squirt boats can be custom-made to a paddler's weight and size so that they fit like a glove

Squirt boats were developed from slalom boats. It started when American paddler Jessie Whitmore cut down several old slalom boats making them much smaller and easier to manoeuvre. Eventually, US kayak designer and freestyle paddler Jim Snyder made the first amazing short boat, and squirt boating was born!

Squirt boats are generally half the volume of normal kayaks. Although they are designed to float, they sit so low in the water that most of the boat and the paddler appear to be under the water's surface.

chapter 4: the gear

Paddling through the heaving whitewater currents requires extremely good equipment in order to be as protected as possible. Paddlers need to stay dry, warm, afloat and visible at all times.

helmet

life jacket

deck

tunnel

A kayaker in their gear. Rafters use exactly the same kit, apart from the spray skirt

Paddlers not only brave the harsh water, but are also exposed to extreme weather. Their equipment is designed to protect them against these conditions and provide maximum safety.

Helmet

A helmet is essential for all whitewater paddlers, as head injuries from boulders and rocks in the water can be extremely dangerous. The helmet must provide all-round protection and fit snugly.

Life-jacket

Sometimes called a PFD (personal flotation device), its padding protects a paddler from sharp rocks, and allows them to float safely in the water if they exit their kayak. It has adjustable straps, so it can be made to fit the paddler.

Spray skirt

This covers a kayak's cockpit to keep out the water. The paddler wears the tunnel part round their waist, while a tight, elasticated bungee cord snaps the deck round the cockpit's rim. Spray skirts need to be strong enough to withstand the pressure of the river.

Safety equipment

A 15 to 20 metre-long throw rope that floats is essential kit for each paddler. Mobile phones and first aid kits form part of the group's equipment.

Waterproof and thermal clothing offers vital protection against a river's icy waters. Out of the water, paddlers in rafts and kayaks wear strong, supportive shoes so they can move quickly over rough terrain without injuring their ankles.

Neoprene Tough, rubber-like, waterproof material

Shoes

These protect the paddler's feet from cold and sharp rocks. They must provide support and give good grip on rocks when it's wet and slippery.

Dry jacket

Jackets made from a breathable, waterproof fabric, such as Gore-Tex®, with latex neck and wrist seals and a double waist seal, help keep paddlers dry.

Paddling trousers

Paddling trousers are also made from a breathable, waterproof fabric. Latex or neoprene ankle and waist seals stop the paddler from getting wet.

Thermals

Paddlers wear a selection of thermal layers and fleeces under their waterproof jackets and trousers to keep them warm.

Paddles and boats are essential pieces of whitewater equipment. Taking proper care of them can mean the difference between life and death.

Paddles

These provide power and support in rapids. Breaking or dropping a paddle in difficult whitewater can be fatal. Many paddles are made from both fibreglass and carbon fibre. These materials make them very stiff and light. The strength of the blades gives the paddler a lot of power. Fibreglass shafts are flexible and can absorb the impact shock from hitting rocks.

Carbon fibre Very strong, lightweight material

back

seat

front

Kayaks

Whitewater kayaks are made from strong plastic. Vertical foam pillars in the front and back of the boat are an essential safety feature. They give the boat strength and help to maintain its shape. All whitewater boats have front and back grab handles to make them easy to carry.

Rafts

Rafts consist of very durable, multi-layered rubber or vinyl fabrics. They are inflated with air, which keeps them afloat. In order to avoid possible punctures deflating the entire raft, the air is held in many separate chambers. They have inflated 'cross bars' that stabilise the shape of the raft.
The length of a raft varies between three and six metres and fits four to twelve people.

chapter 5:

people and places

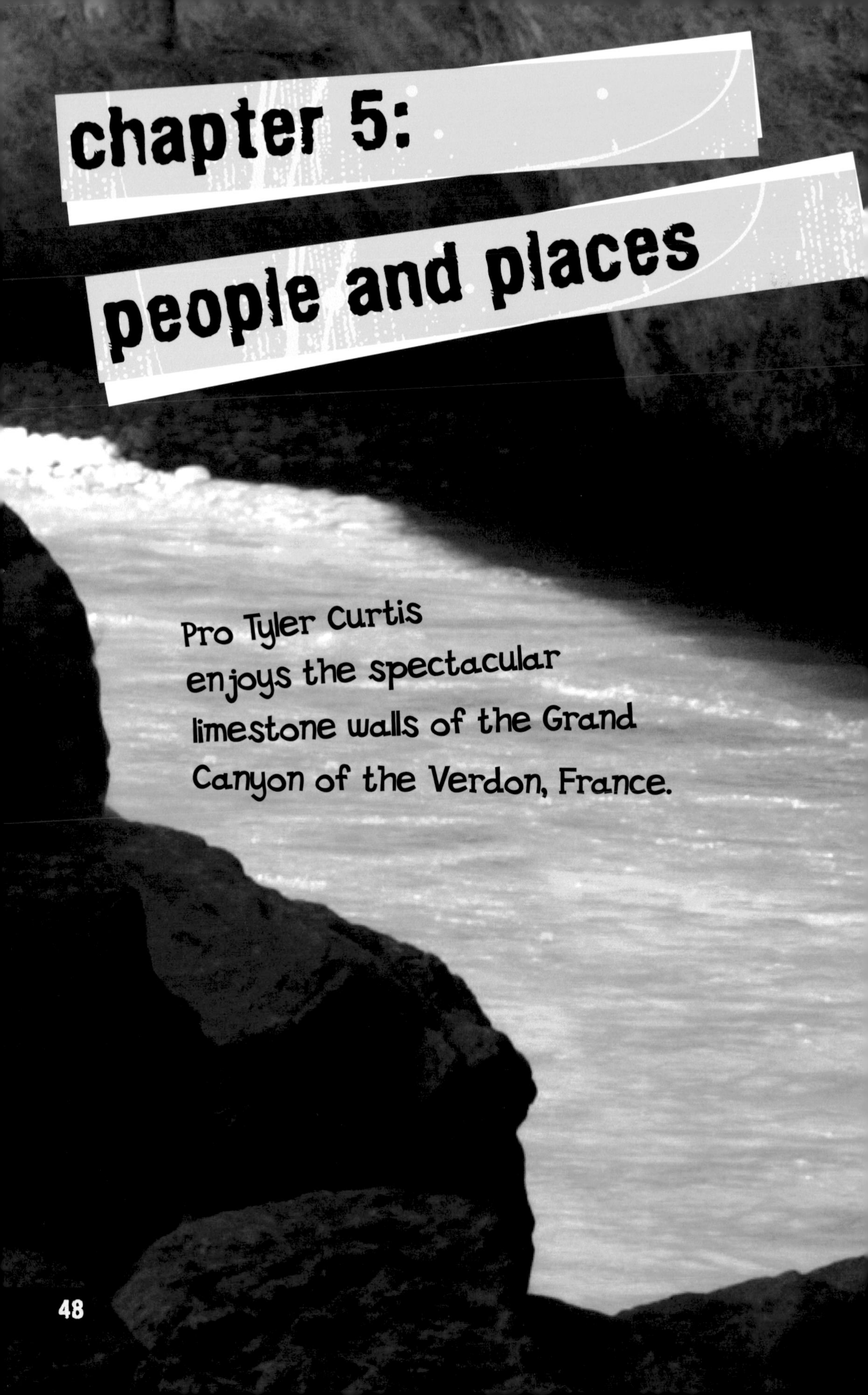

Pro Tyler Curtis
enjoys the spectacular
limestone walls of the Grand
Canyon of the Verdon, France.

Wherever there is whitewater, there is the opportunity for fun and adventure – it really is that simple! Knowing where to start looking for the best runs surely must be top of every paddler's agenda.

Africa

With many big-volume rivers, Africa offers some of the world's best whitewater experiences. The Zambezi and Nile Rivers have become a place of pilgrimage for kayakers. The Zambezi River is home to one of the latest paddling movements called freeride. In the mid-1990s, some of the world's top kayakers lived and worked on the river day in, day out. This elite group pushed the sport to new heights, performing tricks and running lines in big rapids that no one had previously thought possible.

Norway

Norway has to be one of the best and most picturesque places in the world to go for whitewater paddling. With a huge amount of amazing rivers to choose from – small-volume, large-volume, steep creeks, waterfalls, slides, big waves – there is something for everyone.

USA

Every year, from the first week in September, the water volume of the Gauley River in West Virginia, USA, is increased to create ideal conditions for paddlers. 'Controlled releases', which add huge amounts of water to the river in 22 stages over six weeks, transform this river into a world-class 14-kilometre stretch of Grade 4 and 5 whitewater. This is known as the Gauley Season.

Freeride Freestyle mixed with downriver paddling

Shaun Baker is at the extreme end of kayaking, always pushing the boundaries to try something more daring than anyone else!

By the time he was 16 years old, the British paddler had kayaked some 1,130 kilometres round mainland Britain. Since then he has excelled in freestyle and whitewater kayaking, holding the title of UK Freestyle Champion for nine years before discovering his passion for kayaking big waterfalls. His new quest is to find the biggest and best falls, and then to throw himself down them in his kayak!

Shaun has achieved the first descent of over 20 major waterfalls, including some of the largest falls in Iceland and the Alps of up to 30 metres. He has held several World Records and his passion for finding new kayak challenges has led him to achieve more records than any other kayaker.

Shaun Baker on the 12-metre high Godafoss Waterfall in Iceland, 2003

Not just content to kayak on water, Shaun was a pioneer of the land speed record for a kayak! By using his kayak as a sledge on the snow-covered peaks of the Canadian Rockies, he reached a top of speed of 39.1 miles (62.9 kilometres) per hour.

Shaun's most recent exploits include developing a jet-powered kayak. Some say these challenges are not really kayaking, but Shaun has certainly pushed the boundaries of this extreme sport.

Shaun in his jet-powered kayak

Eric Jackson

This American's ability to turn his hand to any form of paddling has made him one of the best kayakers in the world and an Olympic champion. Slalom, extreme racing and freestyle – he masters them all! He was ranked number one in the world in 2006 and has been freestyle champion four times.

Tanya Faux

Nicknamed the T-Bird, Australian world-class champion Tanya Faux is probably the best female freestyle paddler in the world. She was the first woman to undertake complex combo moves, and remains one of the few to successfully attempt them. Tanya has been awarded Women's Big Air Freestyle champion, Australian Whitewater Freestyle Kayak Champion and 2004 International Freestyle Champion.

Combo moves Linked aerial moves

Niki Kelly

Niki is the most accomplished female whitewater kayaker ever! Whitewater, freestyle, expeditions – Niki's done it all and set new standards along the way. In 2004, this New Zealander completed the Seven Rivers Expedition in the USA, one of kayaking's biggest adventures. Niki ran California's seven top multi-day trips back to back, paddling difficult Grade 5 rivers for 50 days in a row. These rivers included Kings River, San Joaquin, Kern River, Upper Cherry Creek on Tuolumne River and Dinky Creek.

Olaf Obsommer

As one of the world's most accomplished expedition kayakers, Germany's Olaf Obsommer has been all over the world exploring the rivers of Canada, Malawi, Montenegro, Norway, Pakistan and Réunion Island (south west of Mauritius). He is one of the most important whitewater video artists and has directed some of the most influential films on whitewater kayaking. One of these is the internationally acclaimed "Sick Line" series.

Nouria Newman, 15, on her way to fourth place in the women's class at the 2007 French Slalom Championships

Whitewater is full of young talent, setting new standards and pushing the sport forward.

French kayaker Nouria Newman started paddling with a local kayak club when she was five years old. Now she excels in many different types of kayaking and has been a member of both the French slalom and freestyle teams. At the age of just 15, she came third at the World Freestyle Championships and was placed fourth overall in the women's class at the French Slalom Championships.

Dane Jackson mastering the Bus Eater wave of the Ottowa River, Canada

Emily Jackson has already claimed the title of junior women's World Freestyle Champion. Not to be outdone by his sister, Dane came third in the World Freestyle Championships when he was only 14 years old. He has won dozens of competitions all over the USA – he's even beaten his Dad! Emily and Dane have both paddled on the Zambezi and Nile Rivers in Africa. They also actively support charity work in Africa by donating some of their competition winnings to help educate Ugandan children.

Emily Jackson demonstrates a Mega-Back Blunt

With Eric Jackson as their father, it is hardly surprising that Emily and Dane Jackson are two of the best junior kayakers in the world. They spend six months each year touring the USA, travelling from river to river and taking part in competitions. Their Mum makes sure they keep up with schoolwork!

N o matter how sophisticated the equipment, kayaking will always remain a high-risk sport. This is the real-life story of three experienced kayakers who were exposed to the dangers of whitewater with near-fatal consequences.

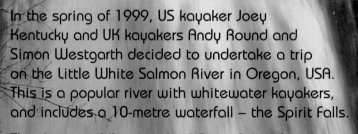

In the spring of 1999, US kayaker Joey Kentucky and UK kayakers Andy Round and Simon Westgarth decided to undertake a trip on the Little White Salmon River in Oregon, USA. This is a popular river with whitewater kayakers, and includes a 10-metre waterfall — the Spirit Falls.

The three paddlers reached Spirit Falls after an eventful day. Joey paddled over the waterfall first, landing well, it seemed. But suddenly he was pushed to the left with the water knocking him over.

Every time he recovered, the water knocked him over again. He continued to fight the water until, out of breath and exhausted, he exited his kayak and began to float unconscious down the river.

Andy and Simon chased Joey down the river. As soon as they got hold of him, Simon gave emergency resuscitation. Joey began to gasp for air. Within five minutes he'd regained consciousness. It was time to think how to get out. They had three options – paddle out, climb out or stay put. They decided to climb, all the time moving closer to help and keeping Joey warm.

Once back at their vehicle, they sped Joey to hospital where doctors found that his heart had too much lactic acid and was beating out of rhythm. Lactic acid is formed in the body's muscles during very heavy exercise, when the need for oxygen exceeds the amount that the body can provide. It stiffens the muscles and causes them to ache. In this case, it had been Joey's heart – one of the most important muscles in the body – that had been producing the lactic acid. The acid had stiffened Joey's heart, and almost stopped it beating. Luckily, the slow climb helped Joey's body transport oxygen to his heart and thereby gradually remove the lactic acid. So it was only due to being an experienced team making the right decisions that Joey lives to tell the story!

Simon (left) and Joey (right) taking a break between rapids, a few days after Joey's accident – he was lucky enough to gain full recovery

Some milestones in whitewater history.

1869 – John Wesley Powell, with nine men, four boats and food, explores the Grand Canyon in Colorado, USA, for 10 months.

1936 – Canoeing and kayaking on flatwater become Olympic sports at the Berlin Olympic Games.

1960 – Boats made of the light and extremely tough fibreglass allow kayakers to paddle over many obstacles. Previously, they had needed to get out of the water to carry their kayaks round.

1969 – Mike Jones, Jeff Slater, Dave Allen and two others paddle the upper sections of the River Inn, Switzerland, known as hardest stretch of water in Europe. Jones was 17 at the time.

1971 – Walt Blackader tackles the Turnback Canyon on the Alsek River, one of North America's most difficult stretches of water. On completion, he stated he was lucky to have survived.

1971 – The first Himalayan kayak expedition on the Kali Gandaki River is led by Hans Memminger. Until then, this stretch of river had been considered impossible to tackle.

1972 – Whitewater slalom takes place at the Munich Olympic Games, with racing on the city of Augsburg's specially-constructed Eiskanal – the first artificial whitewater course of its kind.

1972 – Mike Jones, Mick Hopkinson, Dave Burkinshaw, Glen Greer and Steve Nash complete the first descent of more than 322 kilometres of the Blue Nile River, Ethiopia.

Highest river

The source of Mount Everest's Dudh Kosi River is the Khumbu Glacier, 5.3 kilometres above sea level. In 1976, a team of British kayakers, led by Mike Jones, tackled its treacherous whitewater, navigating whirlpools, waterfalls and other dangers.

1978 – Lars Holbeck and Chuck Stanley begin their 10 years of serious Grade 5 kayaking in the Sierra Mountains of California, USA.

1980 – Kayaks are made from plastics instead of fibreglass.

1987 – The dry paddling jacket is developed. It is made with the waterproof fabric Gore-Tex®.

1990 – First descent of the gigantic Grade 5 Nevis Bluff rapid on the Kawara River, New Zealand, by Mick Hopkinson.

2002 – Scott Lindgren, Mikey Abbott, Alan Ellard, Johnny and Willie Kern, Dustin Knapp and Steve Fisher paddle the Tsangpo Gorge, Tibet.

2004 – A team of paddlers complete the Seven Rivers Expedition by paddling seven major multi-day trips all on Grade 5 water in California, USA, for 50 consecutive days. Rivers travelled include the famous Upper Cherry Creek and San Joaquin.

2004 – The Source to Sea Expedition ends successfully when an international team of kayakers reach the Mediterranean Sea after spending the previous four and a half months paddling the length of the White Nile and Nile Rivers in Africa.

2005 – The first one-day descent of Canada's Grand Canyon of the 96-kilometre Stikine River by American paddlers Tommy Hilleke, Danial DeLavergne, John Grace and Toby McDermott. Previous trips had taken three days.

2007 – The German kayaker Felix Lämmler sets a new world record for free fall kayaking down a waterfall. He descends a dramatic 34 metres down the Leuenfall Waterfall, Switzerland.

All in a day

In 2005, The Upper Cherry Creek in California, USA, is completed by American paddlers in just one day. They complete the arduous 18-kilometre hike in 5 hours, setting off at 3am. This is then followed by 6 ½ hours of paddling on Grade 5 rapids. Previous attempts had taken one day to hike in and two days to paddle out.

Glossary

Blade The wide piece at the end of a paddle used to push against the water.

Boil A pressurised section of water, often where two currents meet.

Bow The front of a boat.

Broach To become caught against an obstruction and turned sideways by the current. A very dangerous situation.

Canoe A light, narrow, open boat propelled by one or more paddlers in a kneeling position. Canoeists use single-bladed paddles, alternating strokes from one side of the canoe to the other. Canoes are not generally used on whitewater.

Canyon A rock gorge with extremely steep sides.

Carbon fibre A synthetic, lightweight material made from woven carbon thread.

Cartwheel A freestyle move where the kayak rotates vertically end over end.

Chute A narrow point on a river where water is forced through, making the water fierce and turbulent.

Class Another name for Grade.

Cockpit The space where the paddler sits.

Creeking A type of kayaking that involves descending very steep, low volume whitewater. It is much more dangerous and extreme than other types of kayaking.

Deck The covered area over the top of a boat that keeps water out.

Downstream The direction the river is flowing.

Eddy An area of calm water where paddlers can rest, or use to slow themselves down, on whitewater.

Extreme racing Paddling a kayak down a section of hard whitewater requiring excellent boat handling skills. The rivers are typically Grade 5 and involve waterfalls and dangerous rapids.

Fibreglass A tough, synthetic, lightweight material made from glass fibres.

Flatwater Calm water, found on a slow-moving river or a lake.

Free ride Using every wave, hole and current to perform tricks as the paddlers make their way down the river.

Freestyle Where a paddler performs tricks, usually in a static river wave or a hole.

Gate Two stripy poles suspended just above the water on a slalom course.

Gorge A deep, narrow, rocky valley with a river.

Grade The classification given to a piece of water to show how difficult and dangerous it is. Also called Class.

Hole Where water goes over a rock that forces it back on itself.

Hull The underside of the boat.

Kayak Any of the various boat designs imitating the Inuit hunting kayak with a watertight enclosed top. Kayakers use a paddle with a blade at each end of the shaft.

Life-jacket A buoyant jacket designed to keep paddlers on the surface of the water if they fall in. Also called a PFD.

Line The route paddlers choose to take through a rapid.

Mystery move A freestyle move where a paddler uses the rivers currents to submerge the boat underneath the water's surface.

Paddle Used to propel the boat. Consists of a shaft with a blade on one or both ends.

Paddler A kayaker or canoeist.

PFD Personal flotation device. Also called a life-jacket.

River left The left side of a river when going downstream.

River right The right side of a river when going downstream.

Shaft The long part of a paddle gripped by the paddler.

Slalom A contest where paddlers negotiate a series of gates.

Slide Water flowing over an area of smooth bedrock.

Spray skirt Used to seal the area between a paddler's waist and the boat's cockpit, making it watertight.

Stern The back of a boat.

Sumerian Ancient civilisation from what is now southeast Iraq.

Upstream Opposite to the direction the river is flowing.

Whitewater Turbulent water that is full of air, resulting from water flowing round and over obstacles in its path.

Index

A
Alpine rivers 16

B
Baker, Shaun 33, 52, 53, 54, 55
Boils 14, 15
Boulders 14, 15

C
Canoes, early 8
Carbon fibre 46
Cartwheels 39
Clothing 42-45
Creeking 32, 33
Creeks 17, 20, 50

D
Deck 42
Downriver event 30, 31
Drops 14, 15, 28, 33

E
Equipment 23, 41, 42, 43
European Slalom Championship 37
Exit a kayak 13, 53
Expeditions 6, 22-25

F
Fisher, Steve 5, 25, 61
Freeride 50, 51
Freestyle 34-35

G
Grades 12-15, 20, 27, 51, 55, 61

H
Helmet 42, 43
High-volume rivers 17
History 8-9, 60-61
Holes 5, 14, 15, 34, 35

I
Indus River, Pakistan 22, 29
Inuits 9

J
Jackson, Eric 54, 56, 57
Jones, Mike 24, 60

K
Kayaks
    carbon fibre 37, 46
    closed-cockpit 9
    jet-powered 55
    plastic 21, 47, 61

L
Life-jacket 42, 43

M
Murchison Falls, Uganda 26-27
Mystery Move 39

N
Neoprene 44
Nile River, Egypt 8, 17, 50, 57

O
Ottawa River, Canada 35, 59

P
Paddles 46
Paddling style 21
Paddling trousers 45
PFD (personal flotation device) 43
Play runs 35
Playboating 34
pool drop rivers 16

R
Rafting 28-29
Rafting competitions 30-31
Rafts 8, 47
Rapids 14, 15, 16, 17, 25, 30, 31,
    46, 50, 61
River types 16-17

S
Safety 42-43
Shoes 44, 45
Slalom 30, 31, 36-37
Slides 17
Solo kayaking 26-27
Spray skirt 43
Sprint 30
Squirt boating 38-39

T
Topolino 32, 33
Tricks 6, 17, 34
Tunnel 42, 43

V
Volume 16, 17, 34, 50

W
Waterfalls 15, 17, 32, 33, 50, 52,
Waves
    high 14, 15, 17, 50
    medium-sized 14
    play runs 35
    small 14
Whirlpools 14, 15
World Freestyle Championships
    35, 56
World Rafting Championships 30

Z
Zambezi River 5, 17, 29, 31,
    50, 57